MidWest CowPoke

By

Trae Q L Venerable

www.traevenerable.com

Society says I am not like you.

I ride my ole pony like you.

On the plains where I spend all of my day like you.

Yes, I rope and cut cattle just like you.

Many say that I am not the same as you.

When I walk with my shoulders held high.

They ask if that is an act some form of costume.

Hollywood would make it seem as I am not you.

But when people ask who are you?

I simply reply I am a Black Cowboy.

A cowboy just like you.

-Trae Q L Venerable

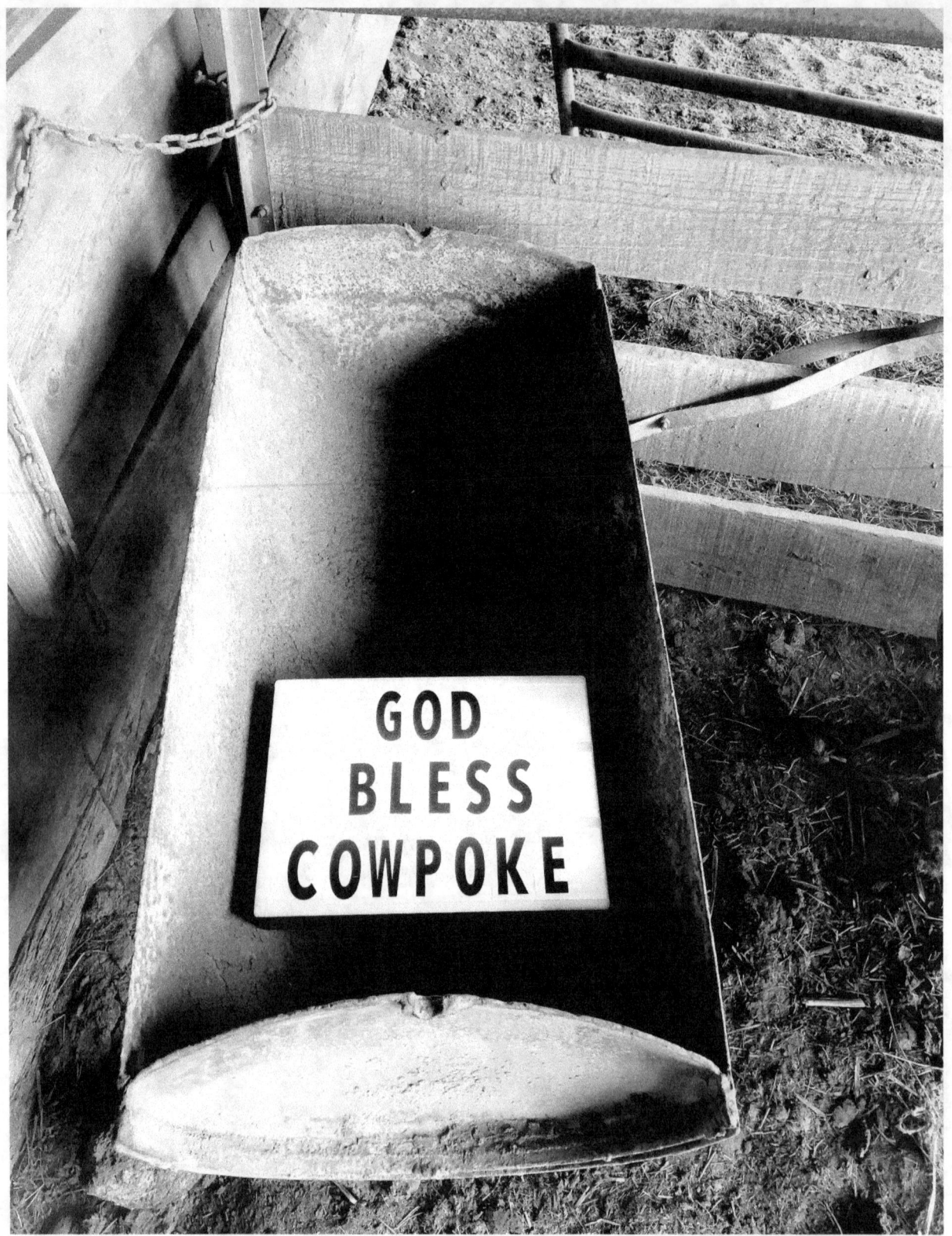

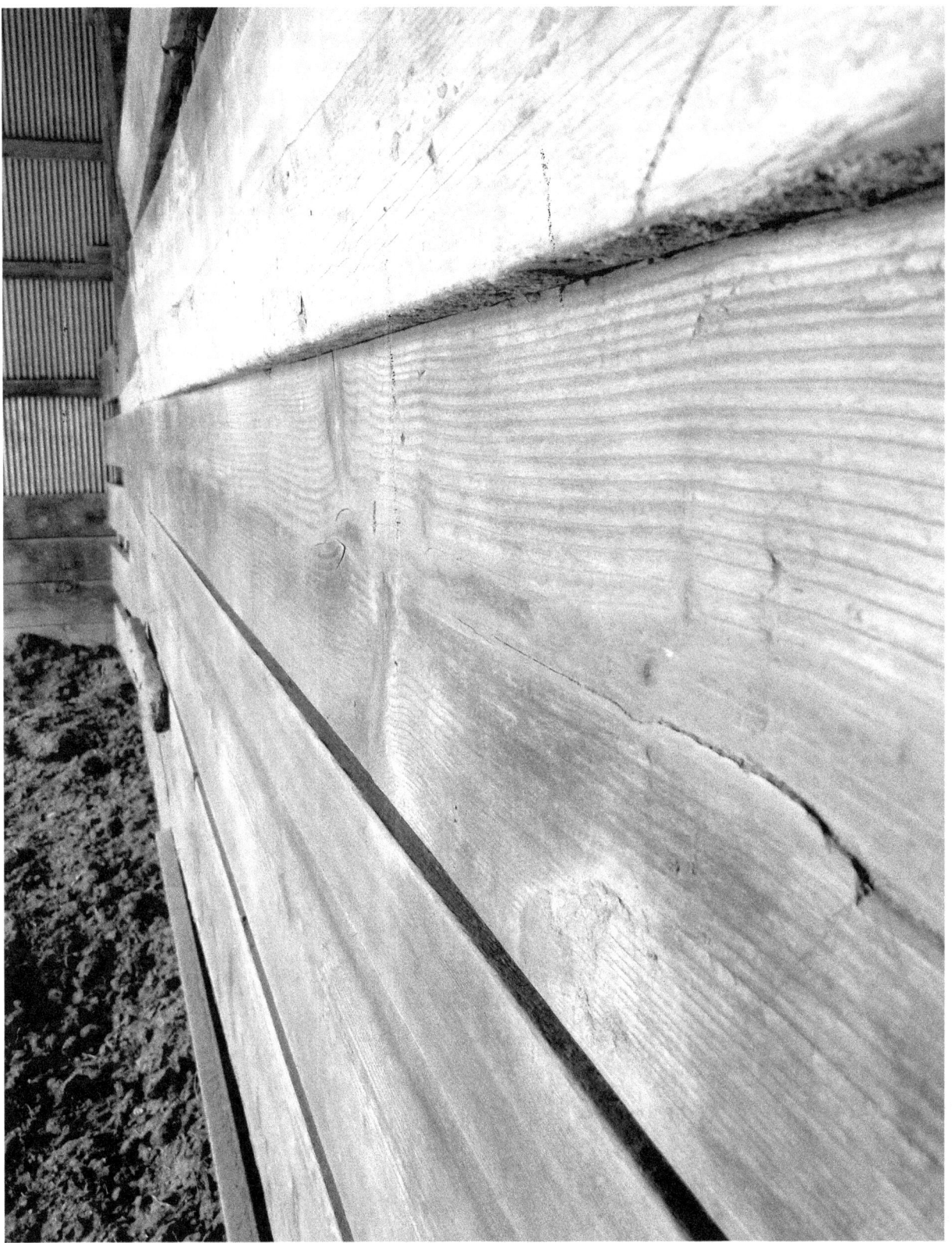

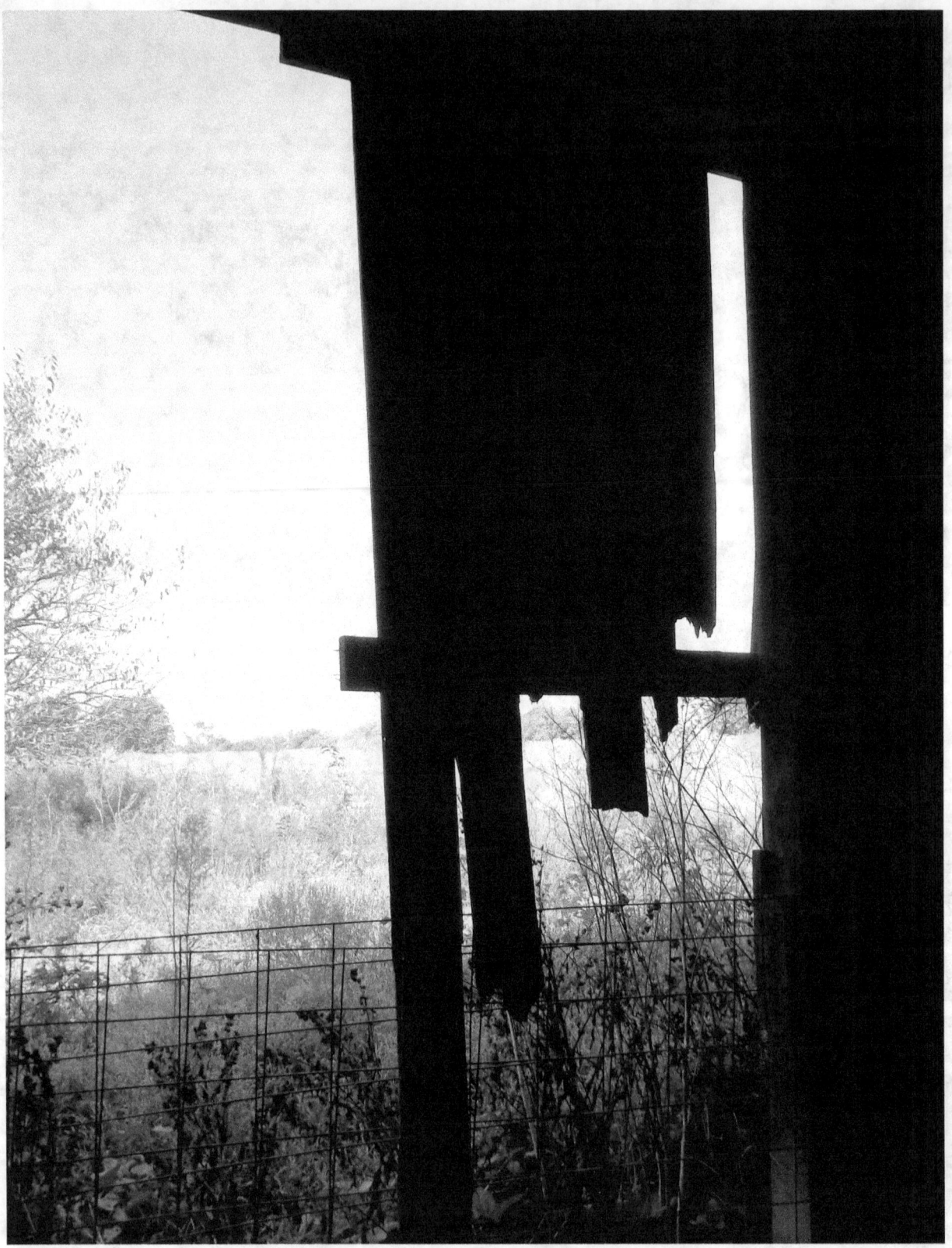

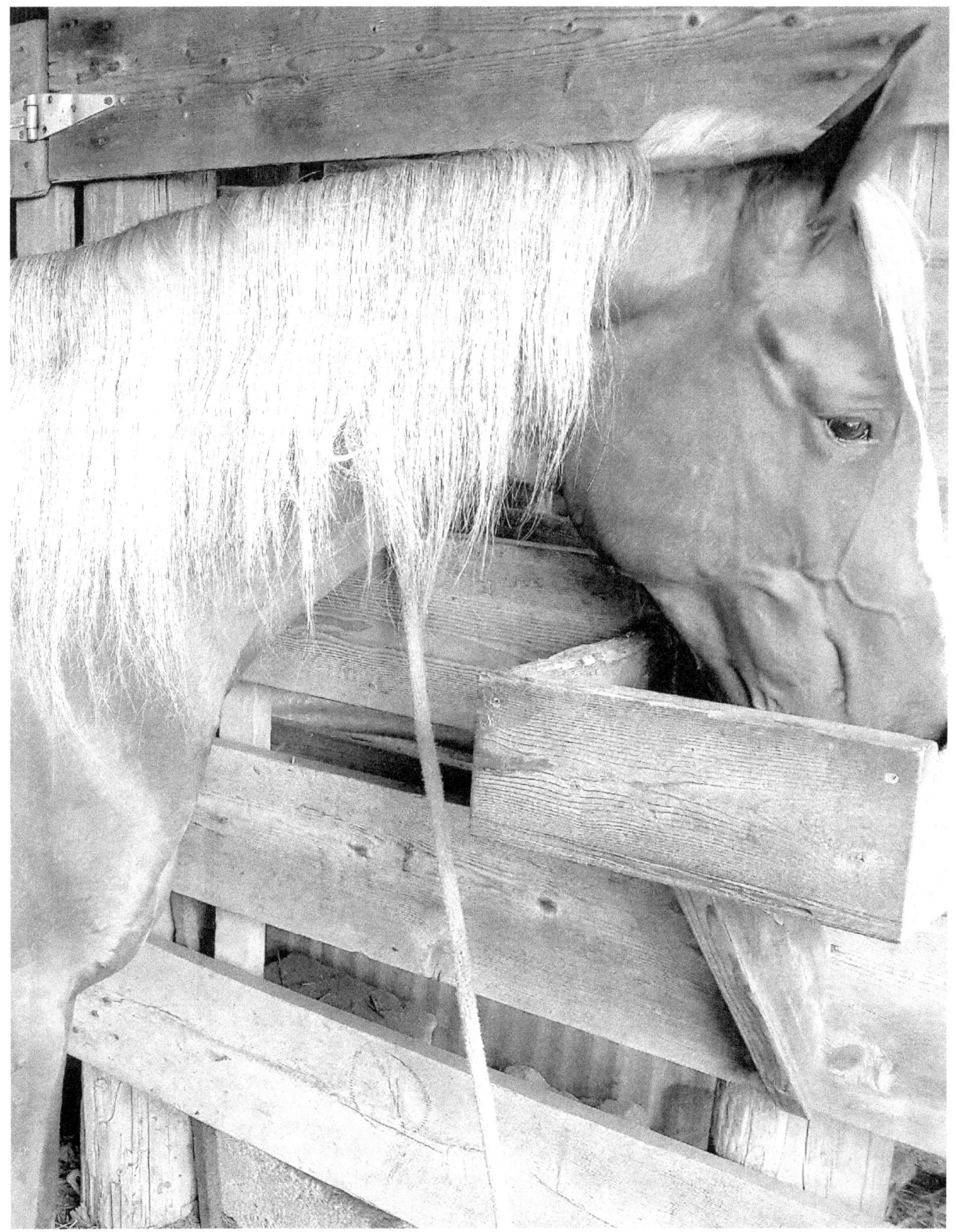

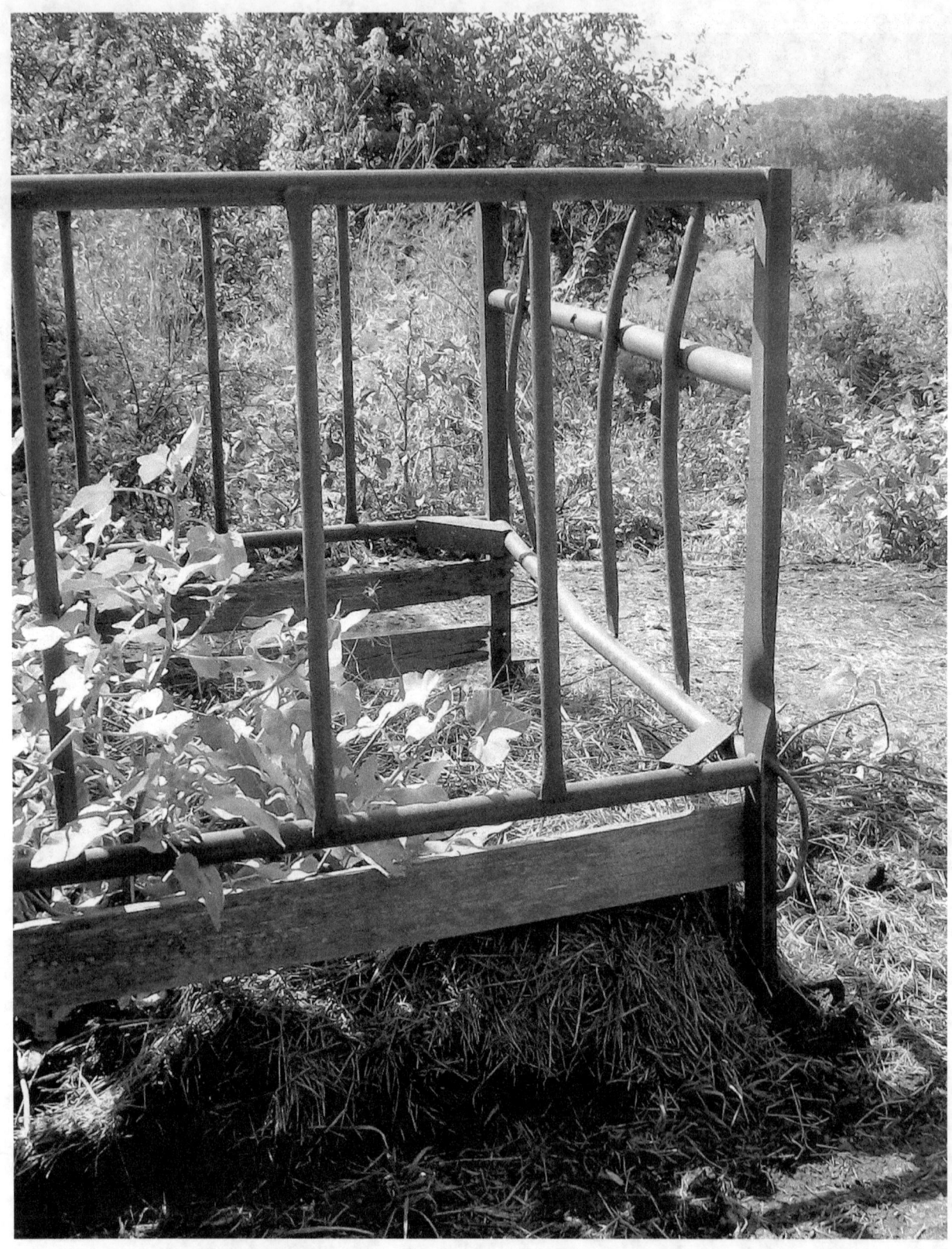

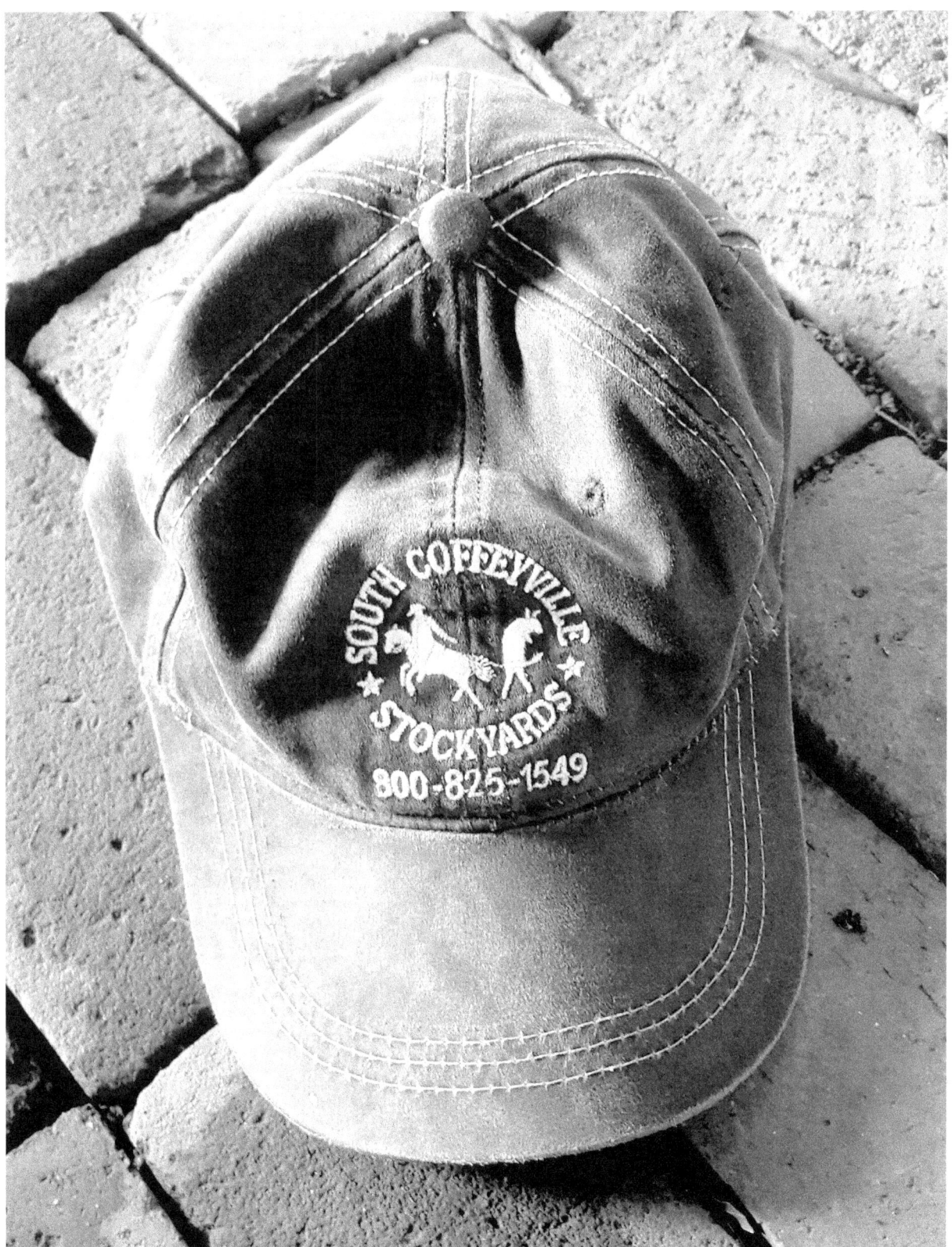

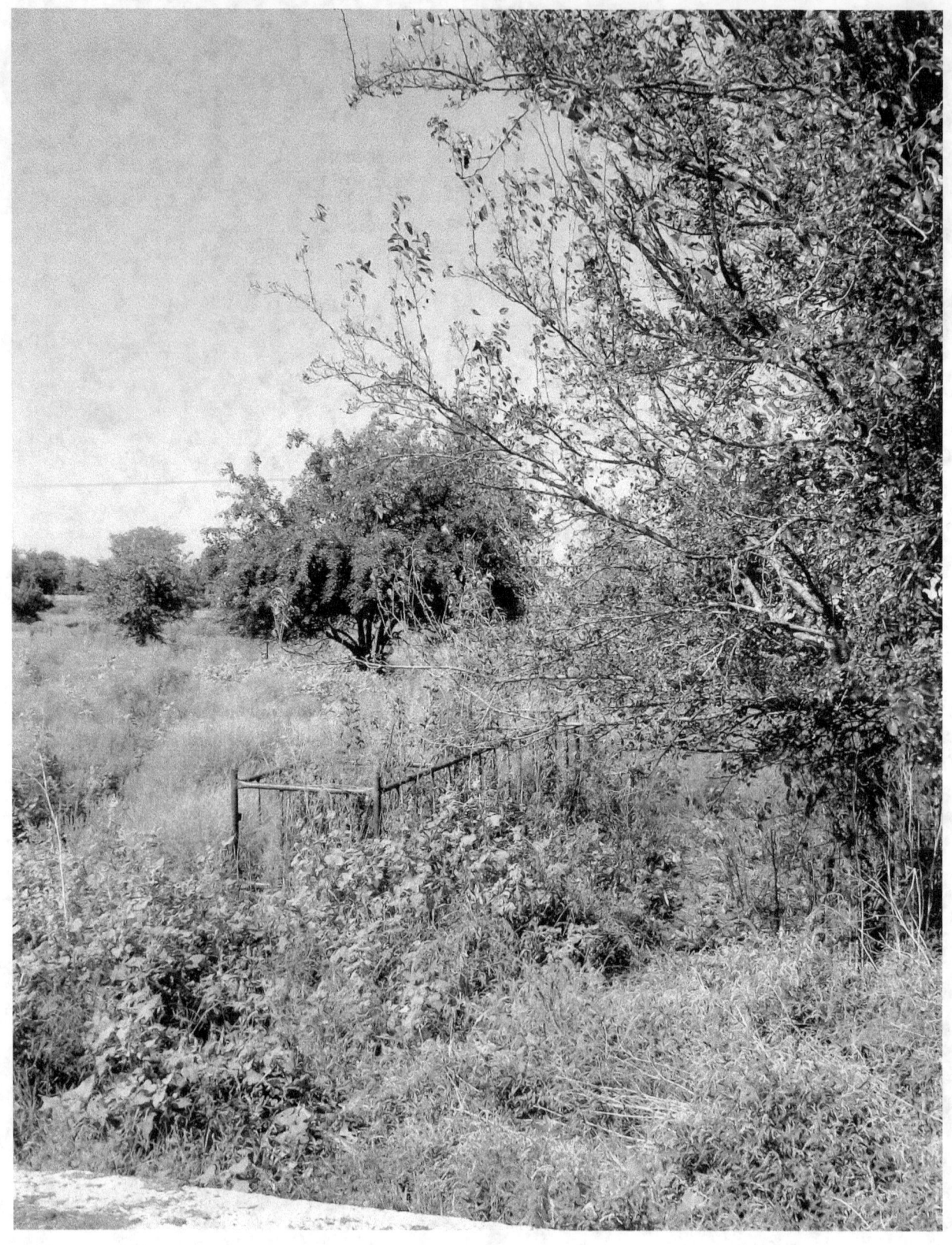

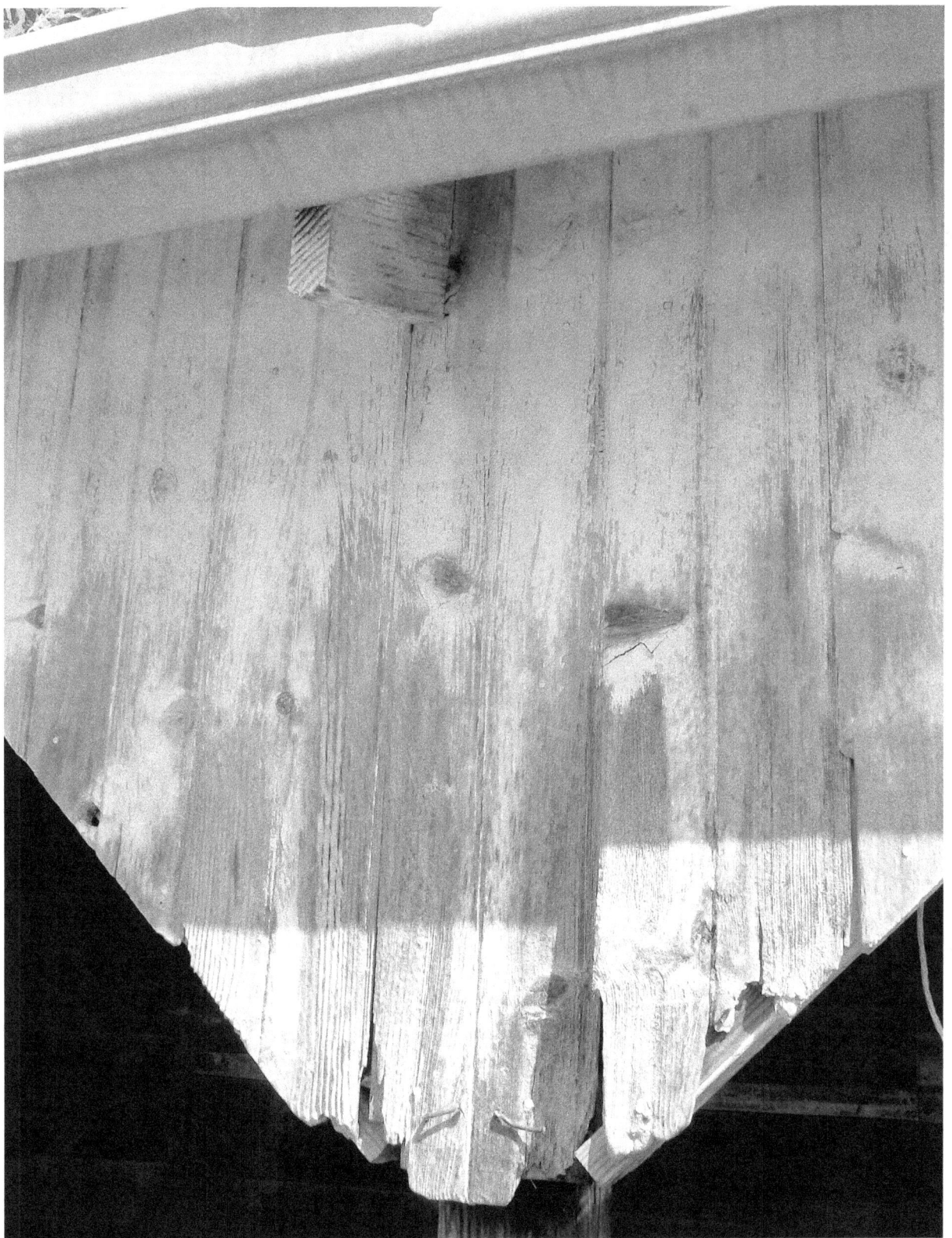

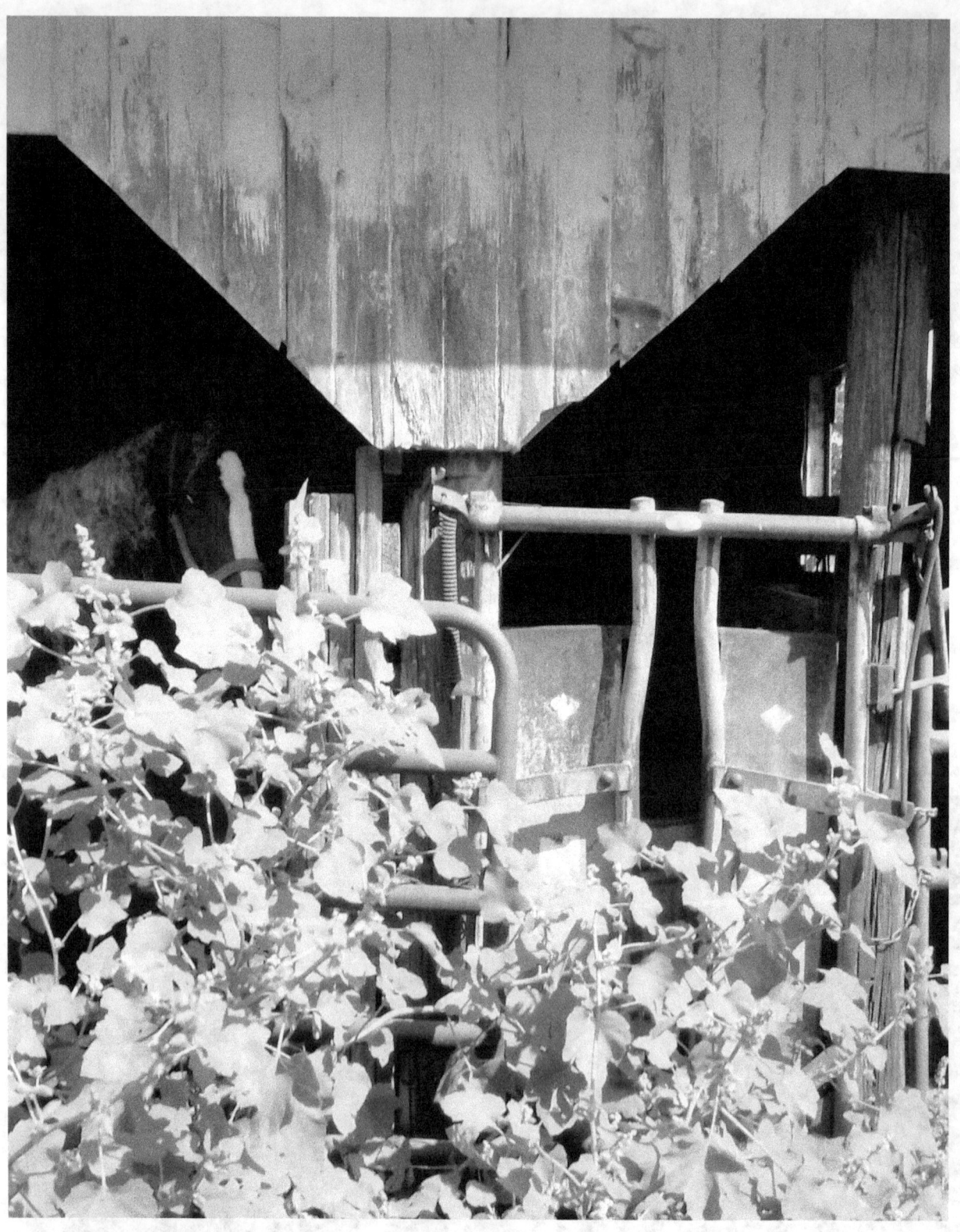

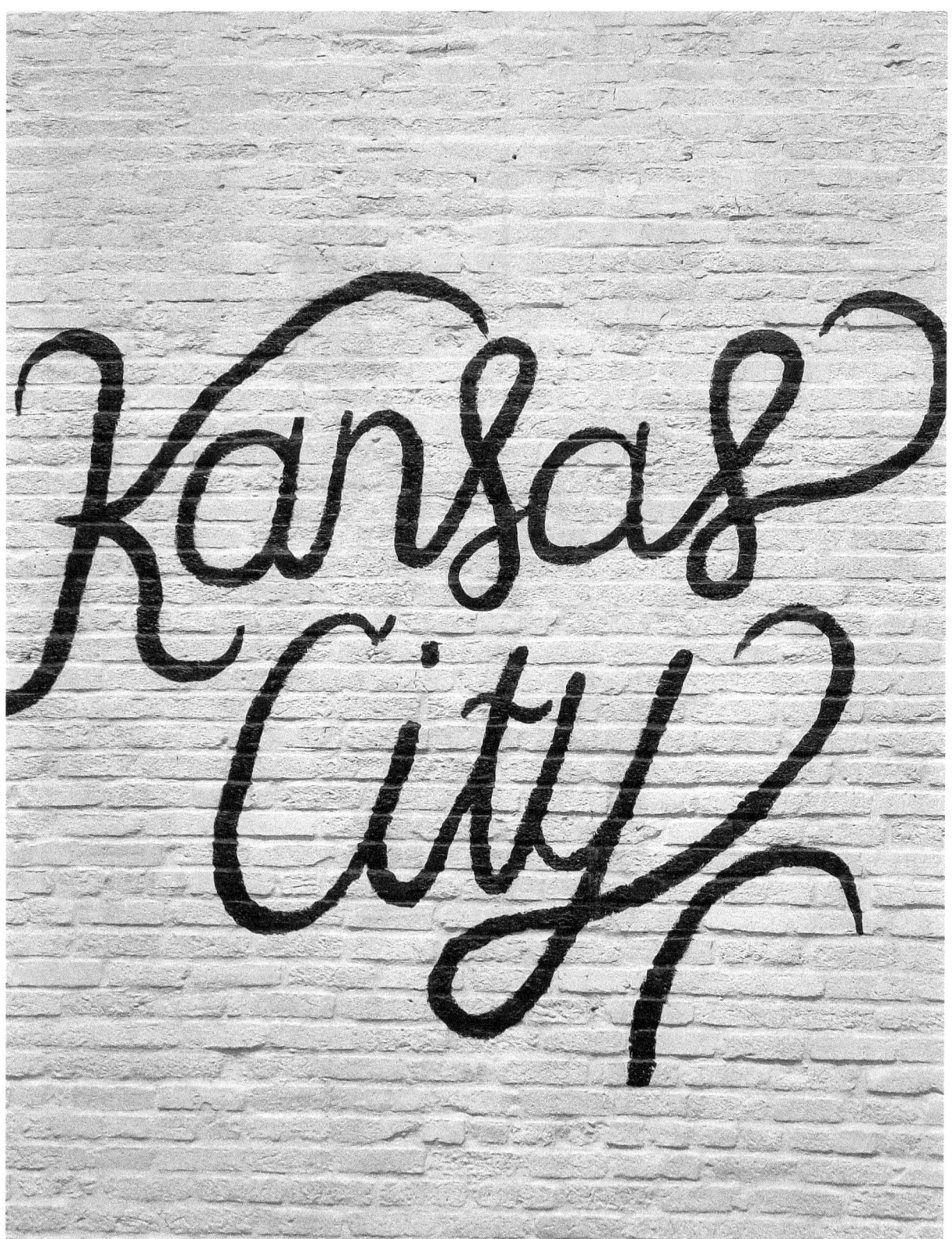

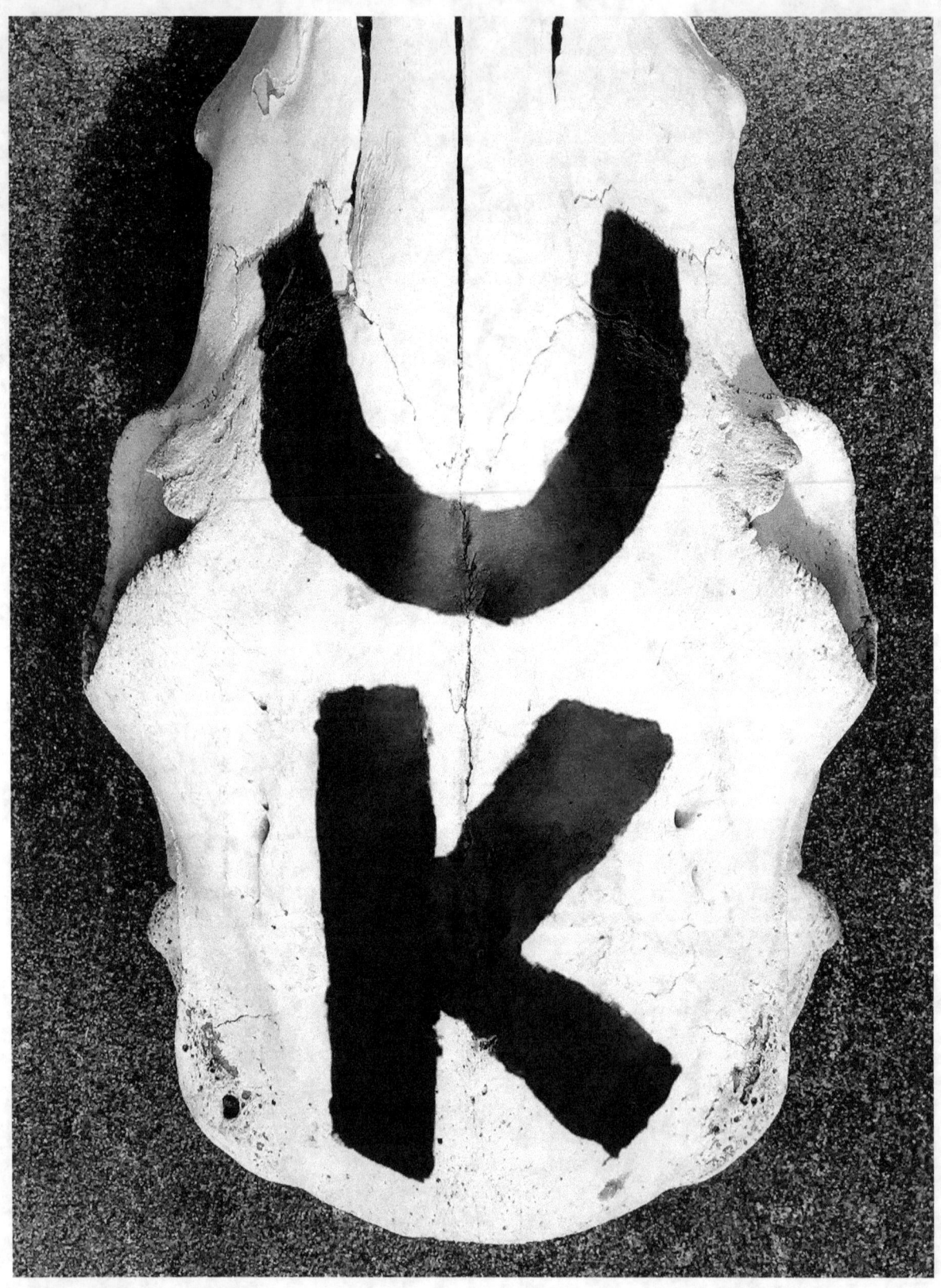

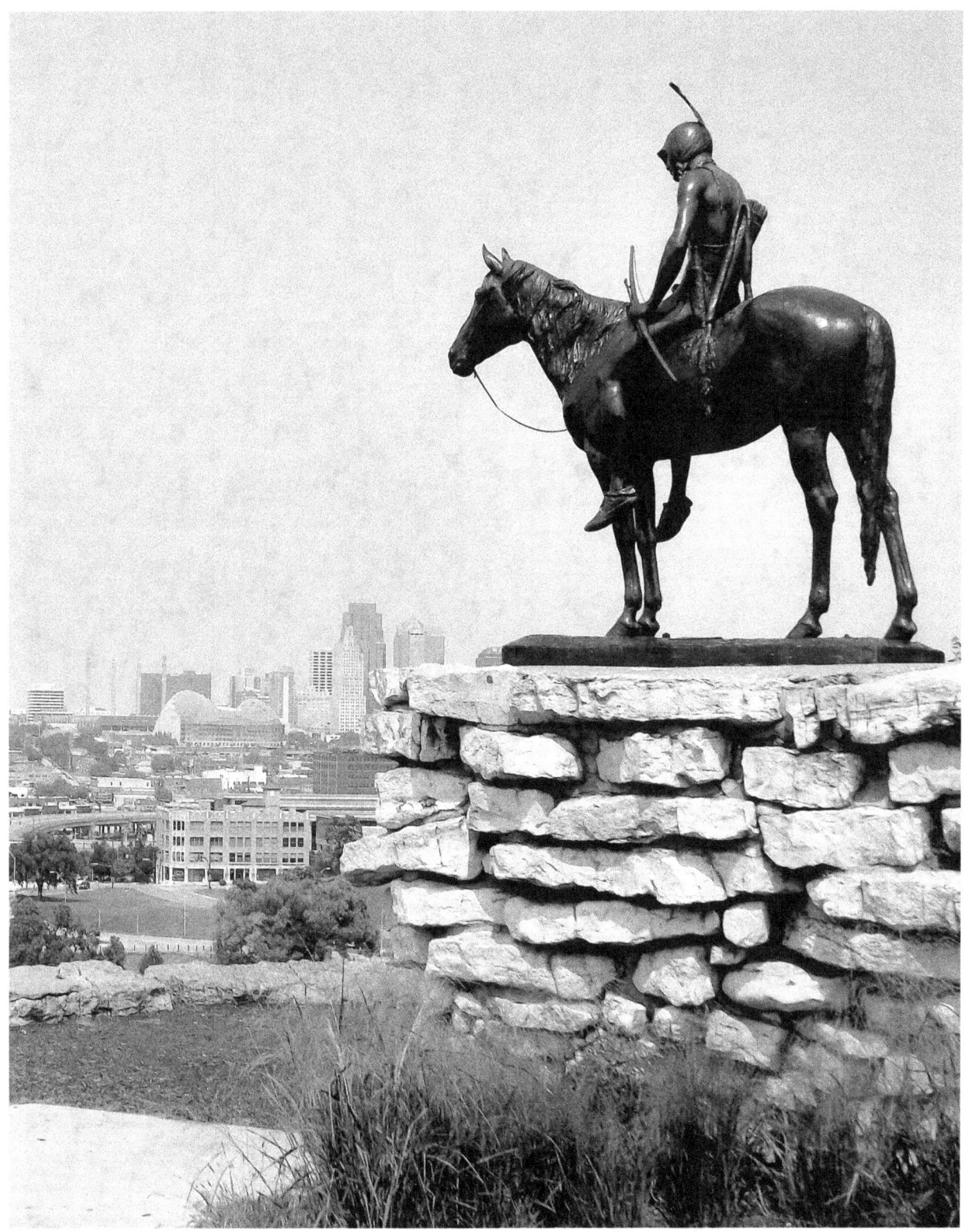

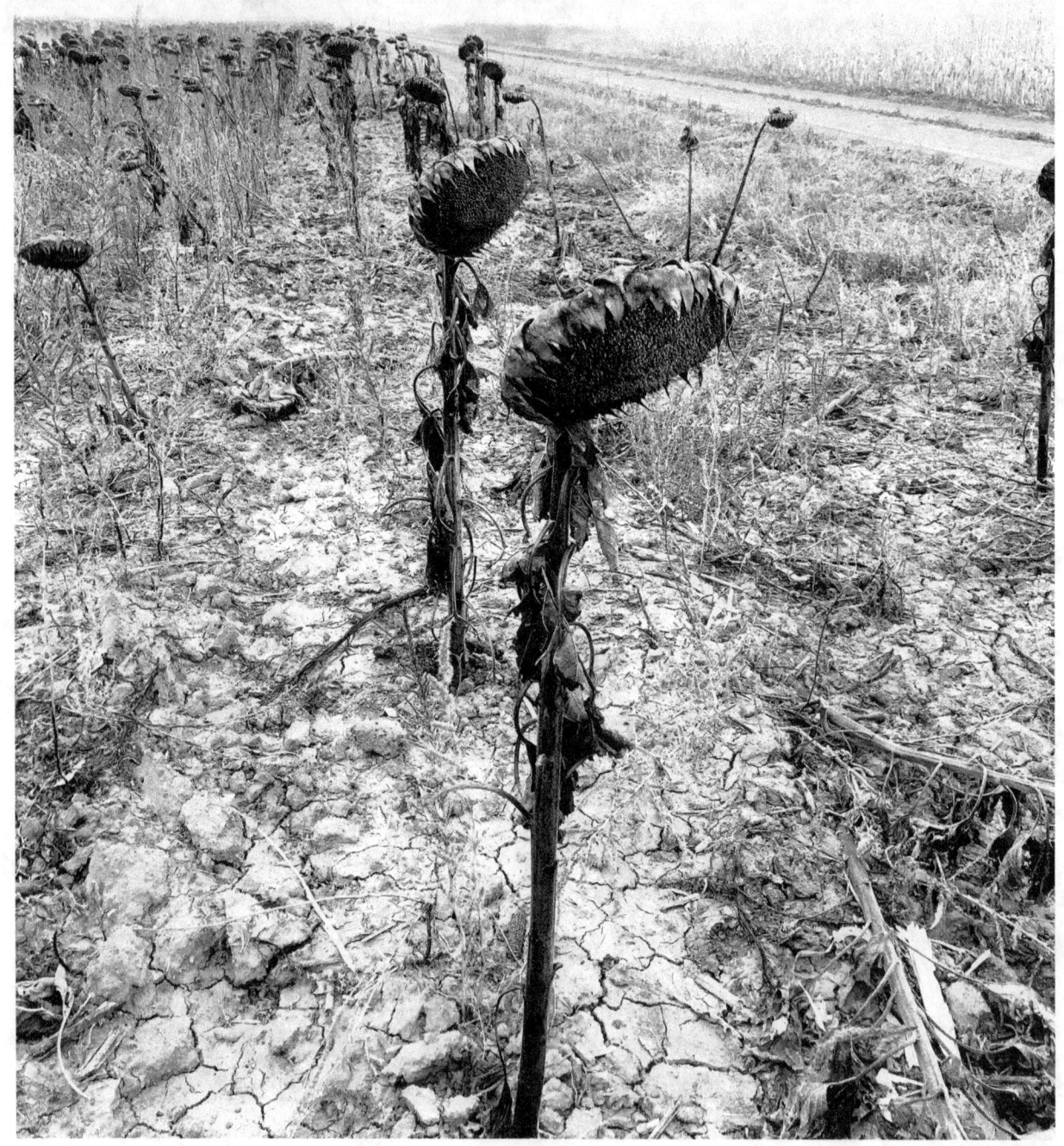

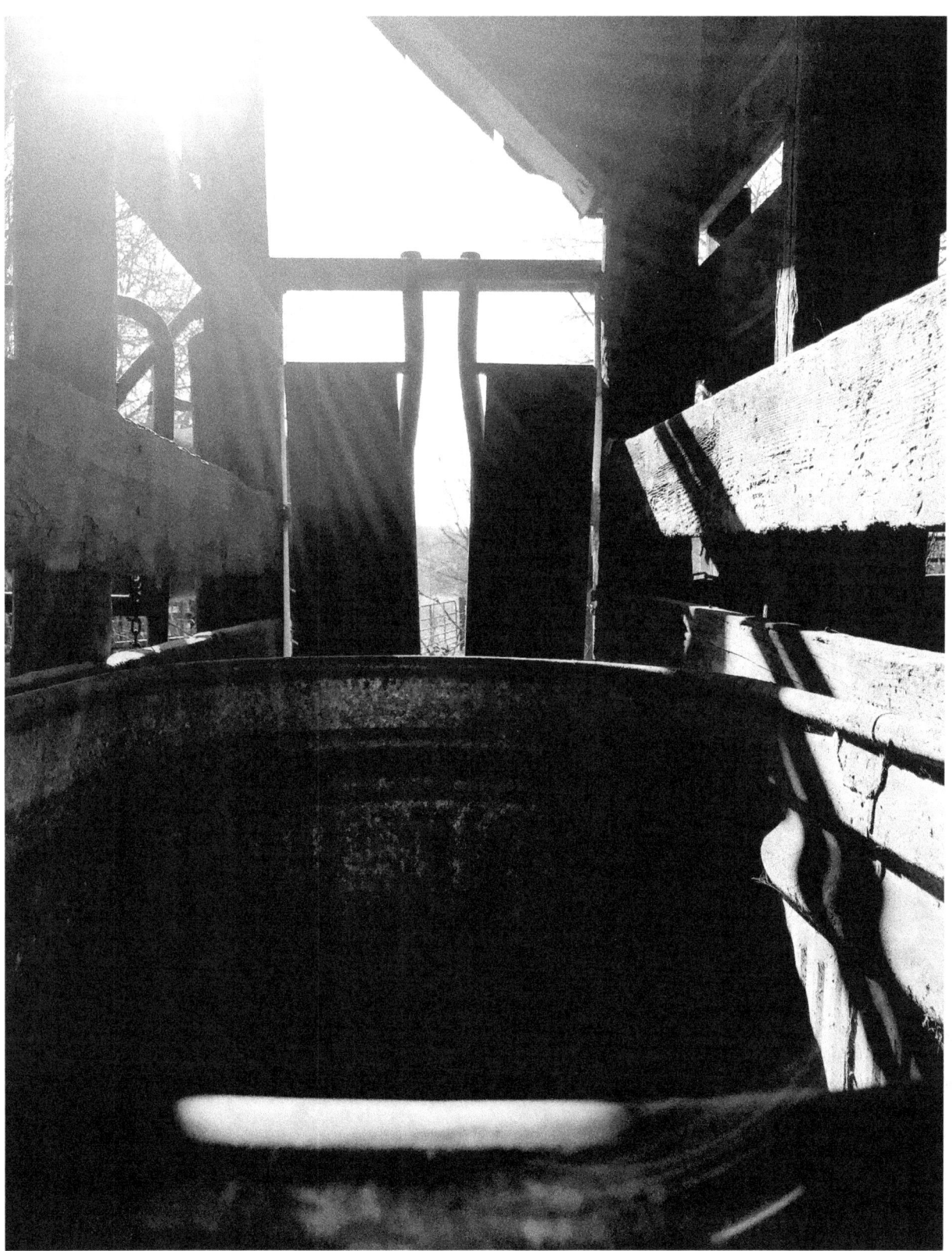

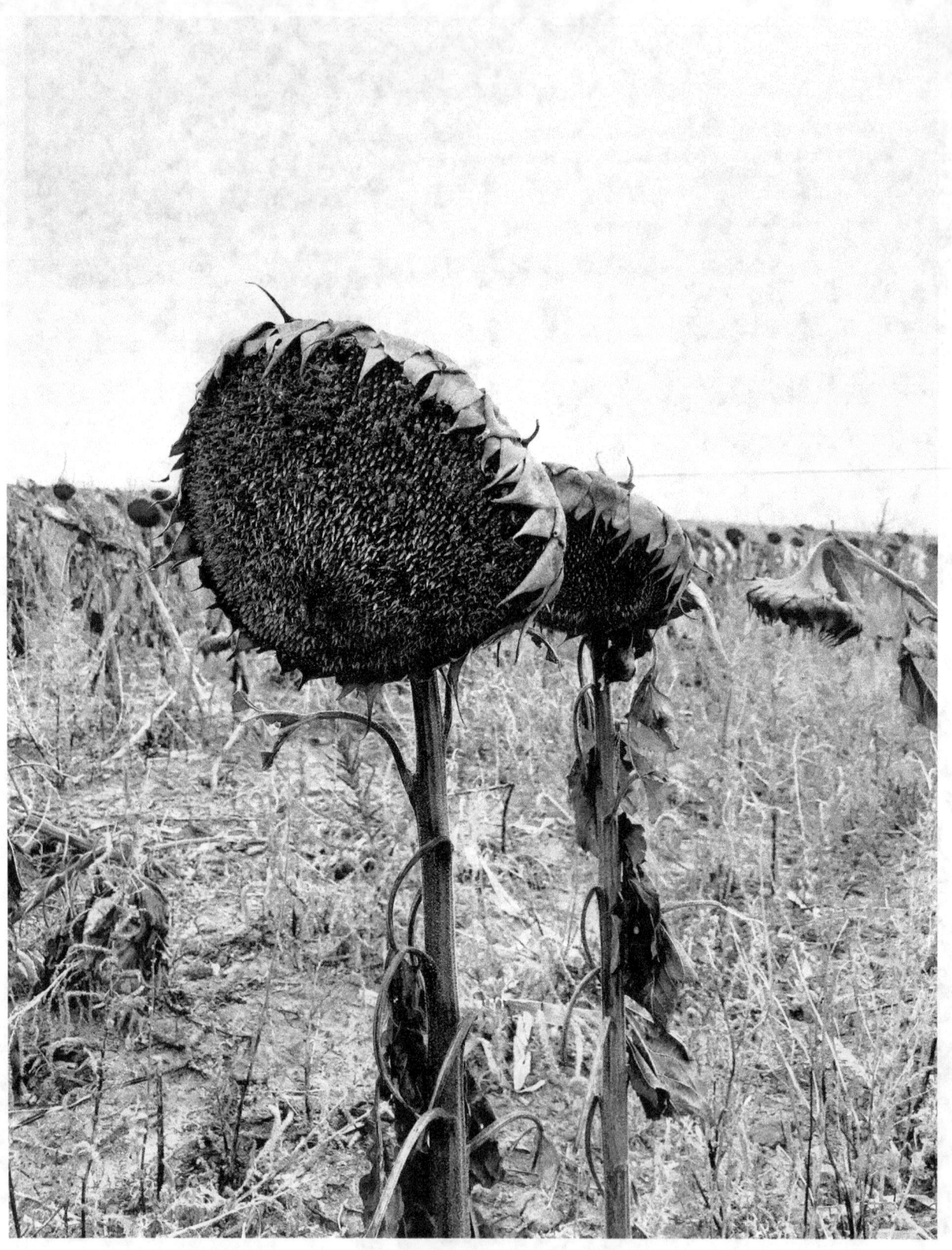

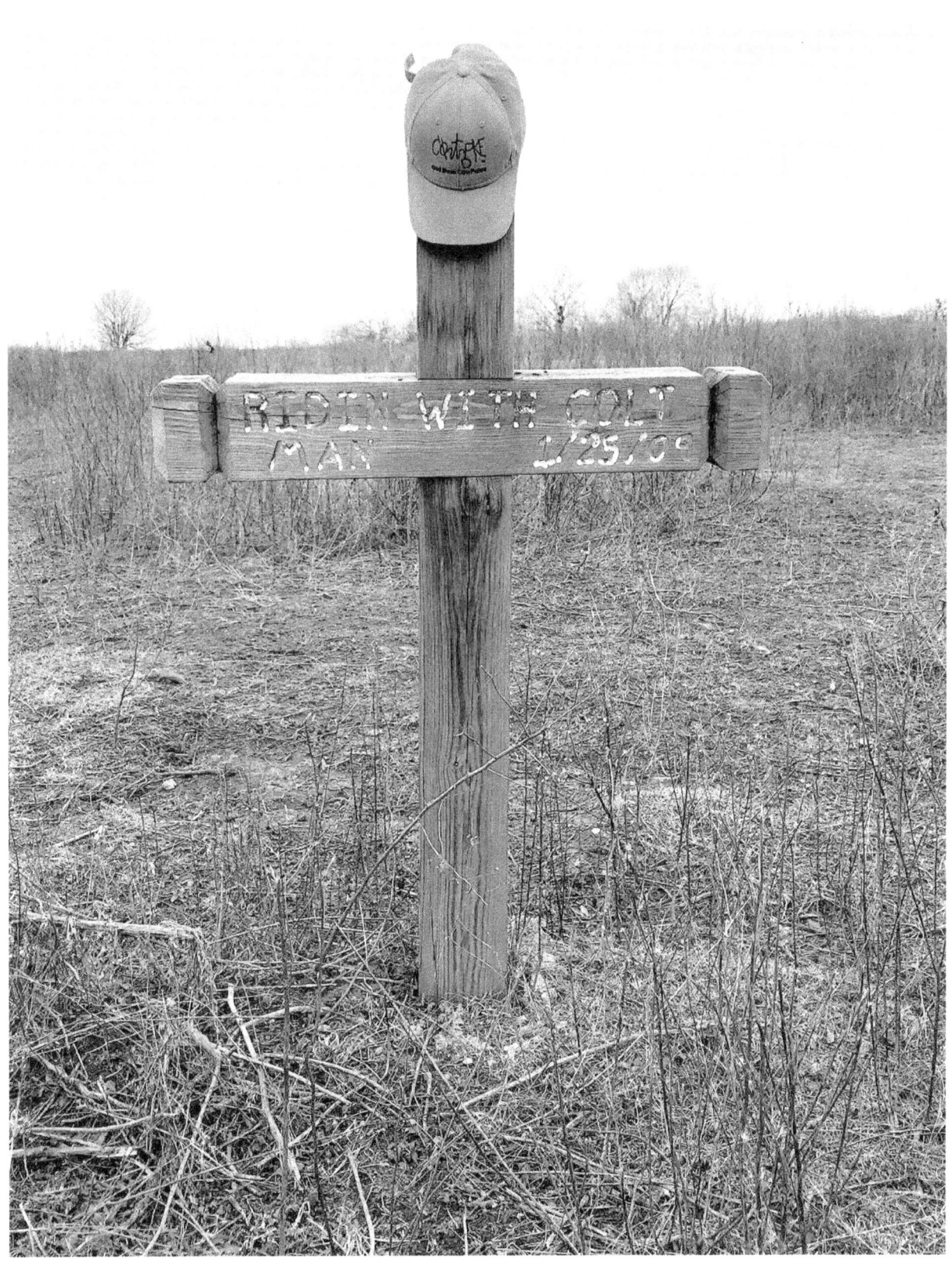

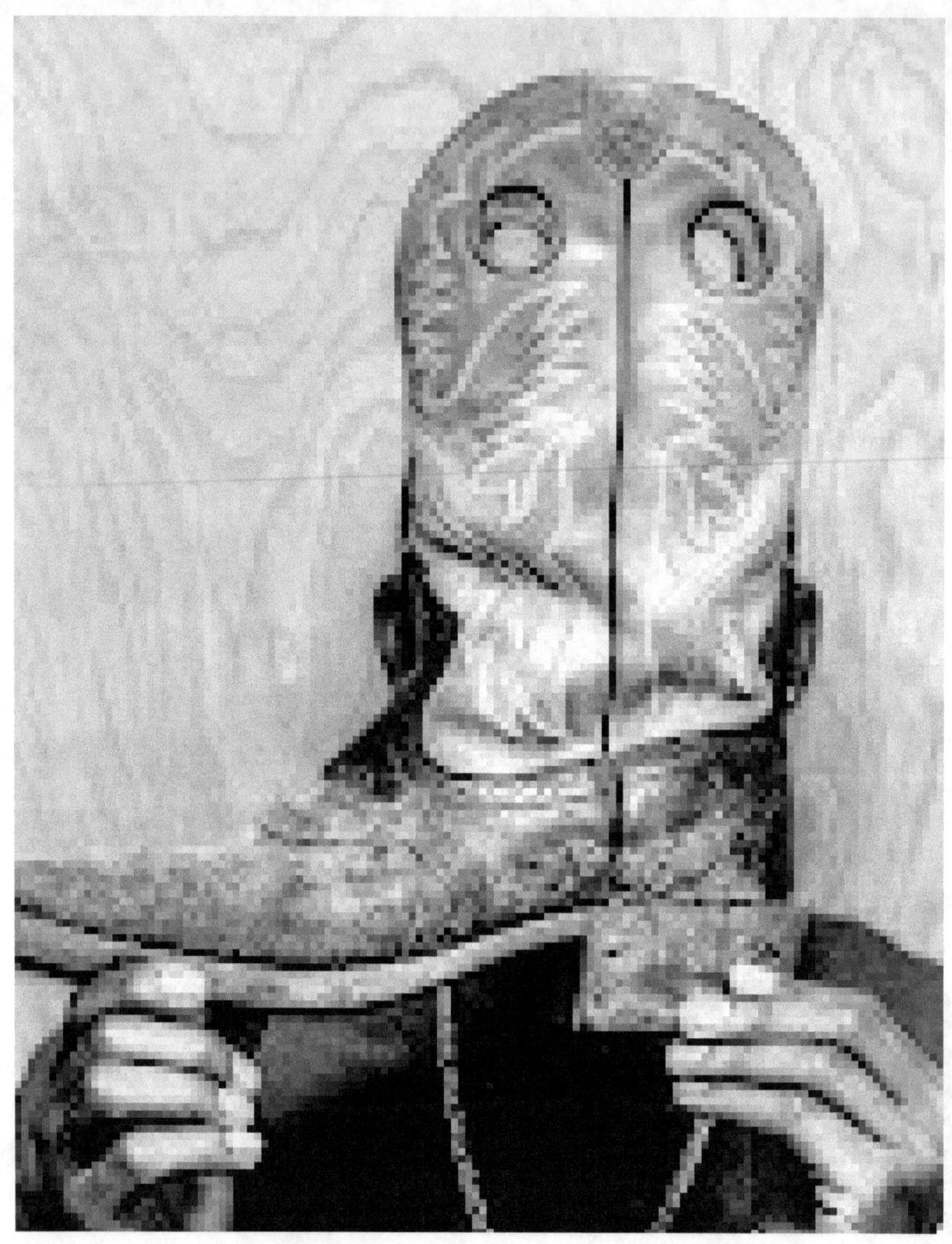

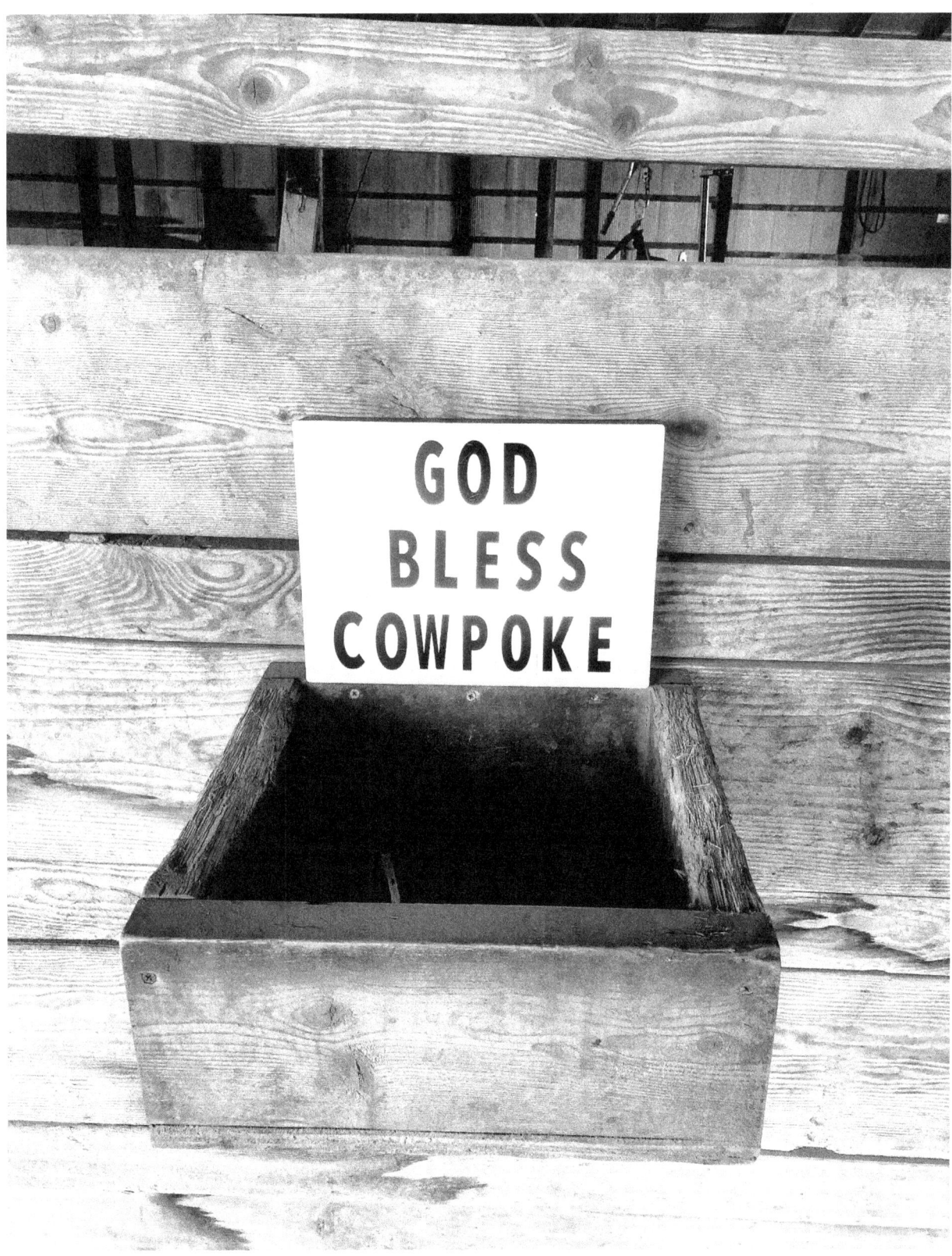

www.traevenerable.com

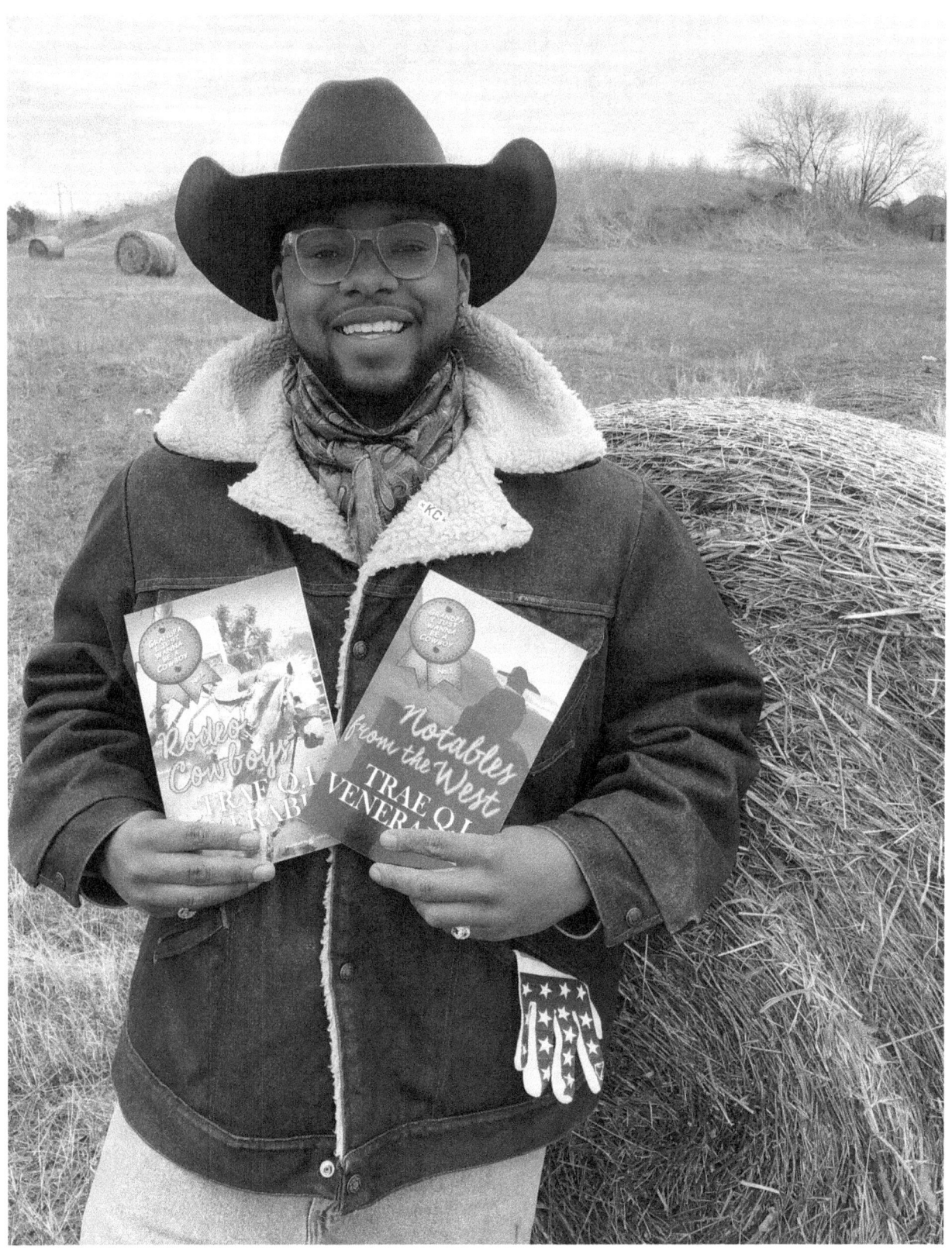